ANGELS
AND
CHERUBS

Stained Glass Pattern Book

Connie Clough Eaton

DOVER PUBLICATIONS, INC.
Mineola, New York

Copyright

Copyright © 1998 by Connie Clough Eaton
All rights reserved under Pan American and International Copyright Conventions.

Published in Canada by General Publishing Company, Ltd., 30 Lesmill Road, Don Mills, Toronto, Ontario.
Published in the United Kingdom by Constable and Company, Ltd., 3 The Lanchesters, 162–164 Fulham Palace Road, London W6 9ER.

Bibliographical Note

Angels and Cherubs Stained Glass Pattern Book is a new work, first published by Dover Publications, Inc., in 1998.

DOVER *Pictorial Archive* SERIES

This book belongs to the Dover Pictorial Archive Series. You may use the designs and illustrations for graphics and crafts applications, free and without special permission, provided that you include no more than ten in the same publication or project. (For permission for additional use, please write to Permissions Department, Dover Publications, Inc., 31 East 2nd Street, Mineola, N.Y. 11501.)

However, republication or reproduction of any illustration by any other graphic service, whether it be in a book or in any other design resource, is strictly prohibited.

Library of Congress Cataloging-in-Publication Data

Eaton, Connie.
    Angels and cherubs stained glass pattern book / Connie Clough Eaton.
        p.   cm. — (Dover pictorial archive series)
    ISBN 0-486-40170-7 (pbk.)
    1. Glass craft—Patterns.   2. Glass painting and staining—Patterns.   3. Angels in art.
I. Title. II. Series.
TT298.E15 1998
748.5—dc21   98-21479
                                                    CIP

Manufactured in the United States of America
Dover Publications, Inc., 31 East 2nd Street, Mineola, N.Y. 11501

PUBLISHER'S NOTE

The beauty of stained glass designs lies in its workmanship. Shimmering with color and vibrancy, stained glass remains a popular and attractive decoration with tons of uses. The sixty patterns in this book all depict enchanting angels and cherubs, mostly inspired by Victorian sources. These beautiful winged creatures possess an ethereal charm, and you can use these patterns for many different stained glass projects. Although the patterns in this book are immediately useful, they may also be reproduced in larger or smaller sizes. Use your creativity to imagine an unlimited number of applications for these versatile designs. The graceful innocence of these angels and cherubs will add a heavenly touch to any arts and crafts project.

This collection of patterns is intended as a supplement to stained glass instruction books (such as *Stained Glass Craft* by J. A. F. Divine and G. Blachford, Dover Publications, Inc., 0-486-22812-6). All materials needed, including general instructions and tools for beginners, can usually be purchased from local craft and hobby stores listed in your Yellow Pages.

Cherub and cornucopia of flowers, from Victorian card.

1

Loving angels, from Victorian valentine.

Cherub with garland, from Victorian valentine.

3

Cherubs among the flowers, from Victorian card.

Cherub with garland, from Victorian valentine.

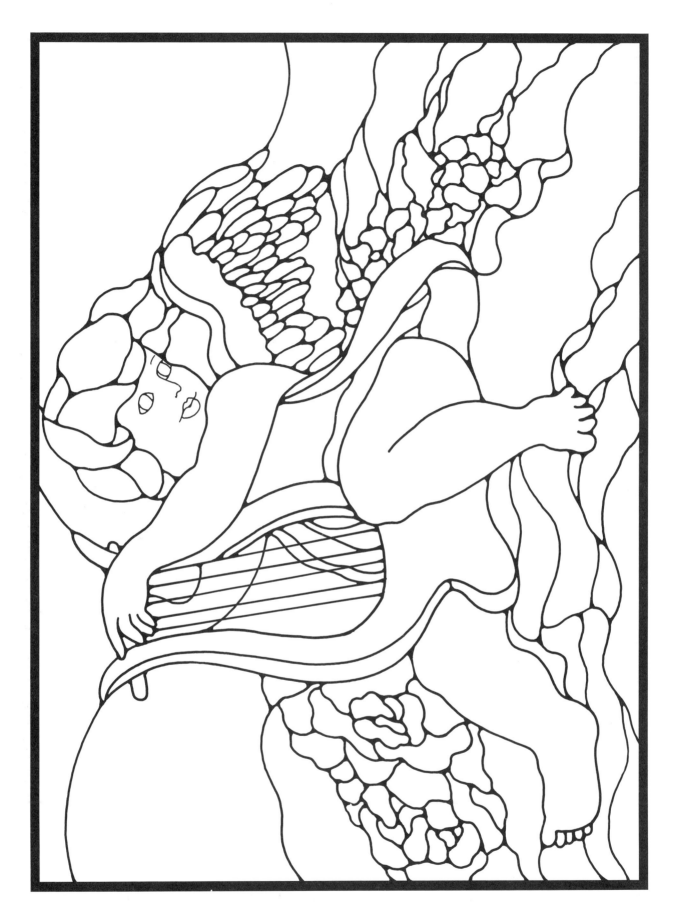

Cherub with harp, from 19th-century wood engraving.

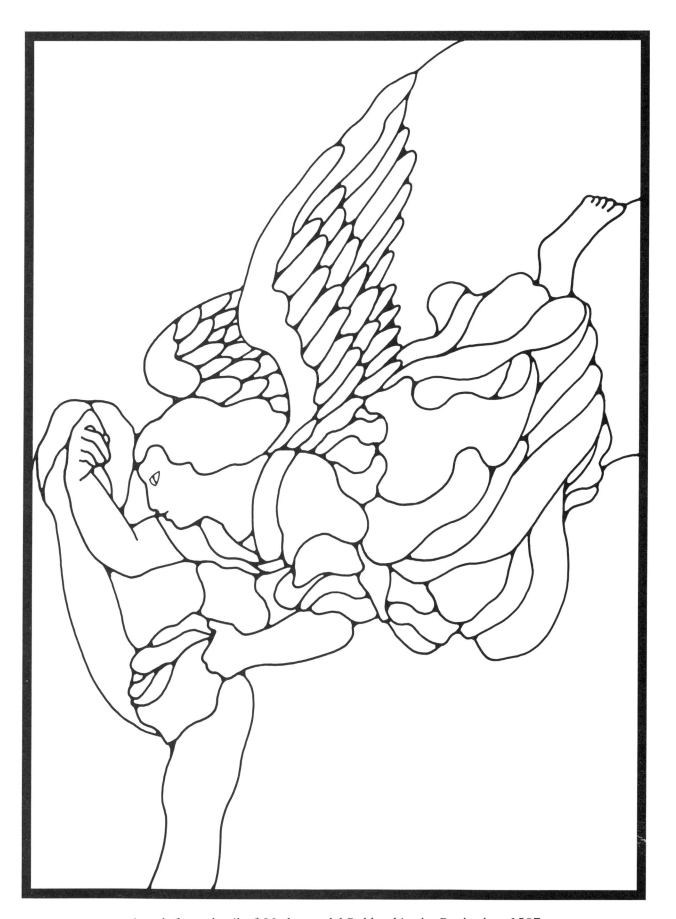

Angel, from detail of *Madonna del Baldacchino* by Raphael, c. 1507.

Angel, from 19th-century wood engraving.

Two angels, from Victorian card.

Angel, from Victorian valentine.

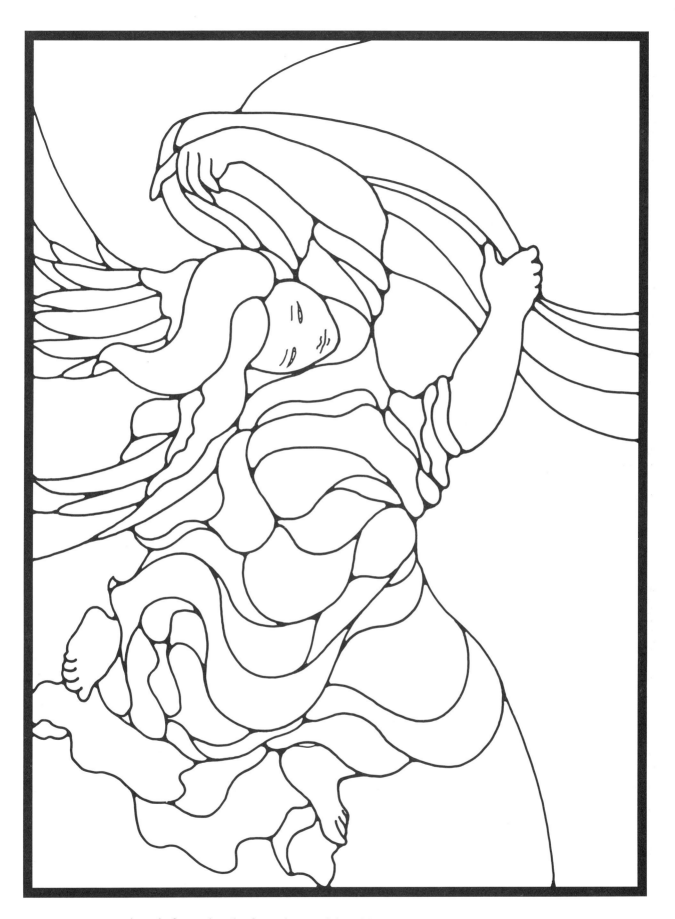

Angel, from detail of *Madonna del Baldacchino* by Raphael, c. 1507.

Angel, from detail of *Christ in Glory* by Domenico Ghirlandaio, 1492.

Cherub with garland, from Victorian card.

Cherub with heart, from Victorian valentine.

Two cherubs, from detail of *Madonna and Child with Saints* by Rosso Fiorentino, 1518.

Angel, from detail of *The Annunciation* by Fra Filippo Lippi, c. 1440.

Angel with garland, from Victorian card.

Two cherubs with garland, from Victorian valentine.

Cherub with garland, from Victorian card.

Cherub with heart, from Victorian valentine.

Angel with harp, from 19th-century wood engraving.

Angel, from 19th-century stained glass window, St. James Anglican Church, Stratford, Ontario.

Angel with harp, from Victorian valentine.

Venus and Cupid, from 19th-century porcelain.

Angel among the flowers, from Victorian card.

Cherub with heart, from Victorian valentine.

Angel, from detail of *Tobias and the Angel* by a follower of Andrea del Verocchio, c. 1470–80.

Cherub with heart and violets, from Victorian valentine.

Cherub with heart and flowers, from Victorian valentine.

Two angels, from Victorian Christmas card.

Cherub with lute, from Victorian card.

Cherub with lute, from Victorian valentine.

Cherub among the flowers, from Victorian card.

Cherub with basket of flowers, from Victorian card.

Cherub with stringed instrument, from Victorian card.

Angel, from Victorian card.

Angel and child, after detail of *The Sistine Madonna* by Raphael, 1513.

Angel with garland, from Victorian card.

Angel with heart, from Victorian card.

Angel with garland, after detail of *The Adoration of the Magi* by Domenico Ghirlandaio, 1488.

Cherub with flowers, from Victorian card.

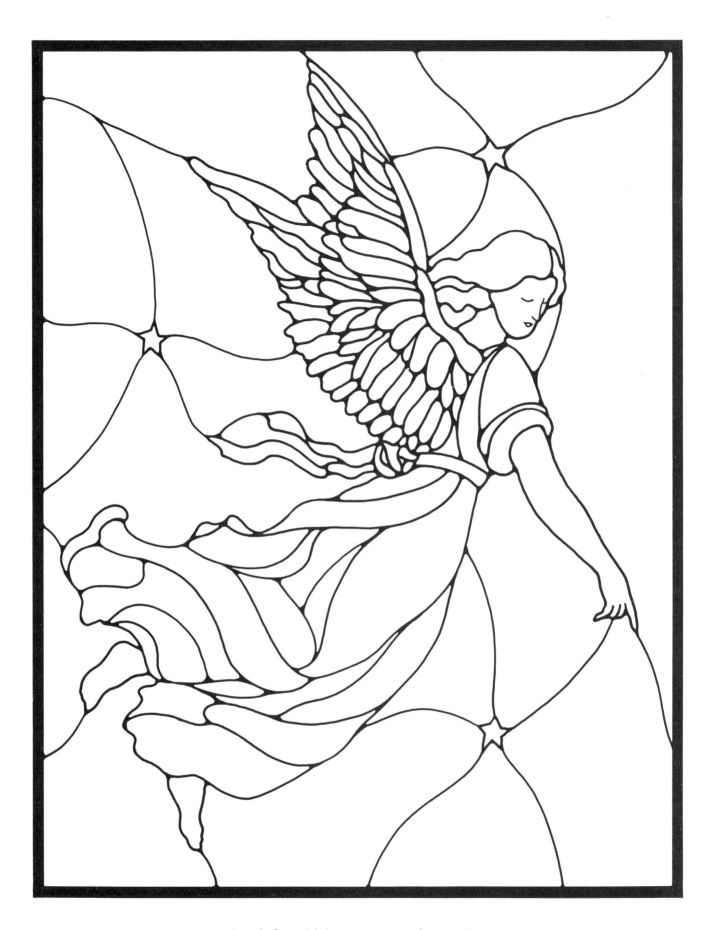

Angel, from 19th-century wood engraving.

Little angels, from Victorian card.

Cherub with heart, from Victorian valentine.

Cherub with heart, from Victorian valentine.

Cherub, from detail of *The Sistine Madonna* by Raphael, 1513.

Cherub, from detail of *The Sistine Madonna* by Raphael, 1513.

Angel, from *Angel Musician* by Rosso Fiorentino, 1519.

Angel on rose, from Victorian valentine.

Angel among the flowers, from Victorian card.

Angel among the violets, from Victorian card.

From *Jacob Wrestling with the Angel* by Edward Steinle, 1837.

Angel with scroll, from Victorian card.

Angel, from antique silver pendant.

Cherub with heart, from Victorian valentine.

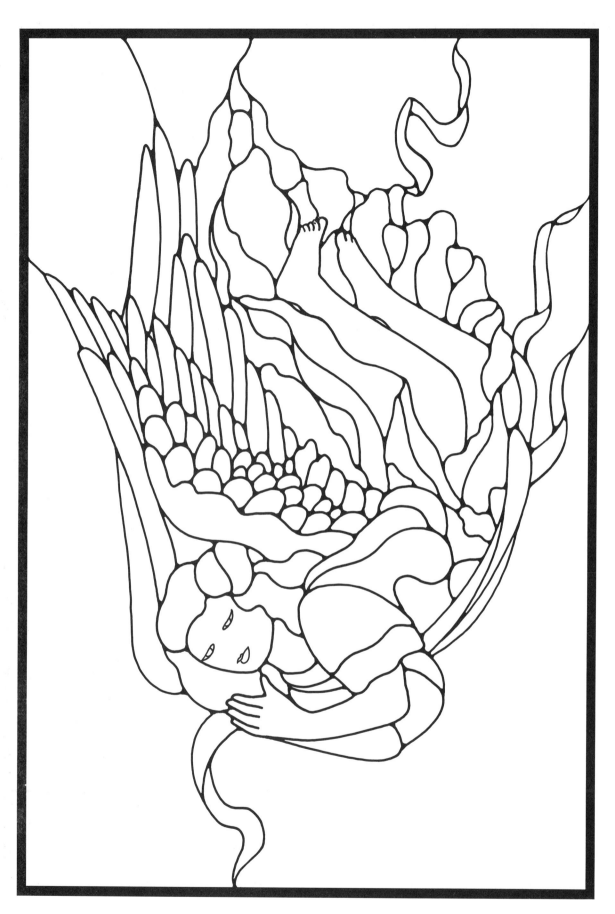

From *Flying Angel,* polychromed wood, 15th century, Musée du Louvre, Paris.

Angel with flowers, from Victorian valentine.

Angel, from Victorian card.

Little angels, from Victorian card.

Cherub with garland, from Victorian card.